About the Author

The author qualified as a doctor over sixty years ago. He then held posts as a junior doctor in a London teaching hospital for two years and passed the examination to become a member of the Royal College of Physicians, an essential first step to eventually becoming a consultant physician. However he had always wanted to enter general practice rather than pursue a career in hospital medicine. Having completed his two years' national service as a medical officer in the Royal Air Force he joined a group practice in the south of England. After thirty years in practice he was appointed the medical director of a newly founded independent hospice, a position he held for four years before retiring for the second time to enjoy golf, gardening and grandchildren.

In memory of Vivien.

Doctor Charles

WHILE I'M HERE, DOCTOR

AUSTIN MACAULEY
PUBLISHERS LTD.

A CIP catalogue record for this title is available from the British Library.

ISBN 9781786297297 (Paperback)
ISBN 9781786297303 (Hardback)
ISBN 9781786297310 (E-Book)

www.austinmacauley.com

First Published (2016)
Austin Macauley Publishers Ltd.
25 Canada Square
Canary Wharf
London
E14 5LQ

Acknowledgments

This booklet would never have been written without the help and encouragement of my family.

Contents

General Practice... 11

Shot in Whitehall 16

My First Patient 19

My Last Patient... 22

Boanerges 27

An Officer and a Gentleman... 30

Never Say "Never" 34

Blood Money 36

Checkmate 38

Coffee 40

Jessie... 44

Mary and Mrs. Gray 46

Neither Christian nor Scientific 51

Renal Colic 53

Scrap 57

Shep 60

Sir John... 62

The Brethren 65

The Buck Stops Where? 67

The Carmelite 69

The Gladstone Bag 71

The Pill 75

Undertakers... 77

Ways and Means... 81

Wrong Orifice... 82

General Practice

I was a GP in a country practice for thirty years. As I have been retired for almost as long, I am scarcely qualified to comment on how general practice is carried out to-day. But one does not have to be closely involved to be aware that during that time there have been substantial changes. Most of those changes have been for the good, as medical technology has advanced so have benefits to patients. And yet one feels that some valued elements of the less scientific side of general practice have been brushed aside by the march of progress.

I retired before the intrusive advent of the computer. Again, no one can deny the advantages that Information Technology has brought, but one hears so often that it has been allowed to dominate the consultation. I have quoted Sir William Osler in one of the following tales where he points out so eloquently that the practice of medicine is more than a science, it is an Art as well. An important part of any visit to a doctor is using the art of taking the history of the patient's complaint. This used to be done by a face to face dialogue when the doctor was able not only to hear what the patient was saying, but to observe his or her gestures, and his face, to catch the expression of pain, grief, frustration or relief written on it, to sympathise, comfort and endeavour to reassure when necessary. This is now more difficult as "half the time the doctor is looking at the computer and not listening to what I am saying", is not an uncommon complaint.

For decades, generations, a medical consultation has taken the form of identifying the complaint, taking a history of the symptoms, followed by a physical examination and then, if considered necessary, a test or investigation to help to confirm the provisional diagnosis. The history was considered so important that many old physicians maintained that if, after taking it, one was not able to have at least a good idea of the probable diagnosis, it was unlikely that the subsequent examination was going to give it to you. Nevertheless, the physical examination; the physical contact between the patient and practitioner, helped to promote a completely asexual intimacy which enhanced confidence and the special confidential relationship which was considered to be so valuable. It is probably even more relevant in the relationship between patient and nurse, when the nurse has to be in close physical contact with her patient when providing intimate treatment. One has the feeling that this time honoured sequence of events in a consultation has now been cut short or replaced by technology. Why take ten or fifteen minutes in a busy surgery palpating an abdomen trying to feel for any abnormality, or to identify the nature of a lump, when a referral to the hospital for a scan will give you the answer, accurately, in a few minutes?

Visiting a patient in his or her home used to be considered the jewel in the crown of British medical practice. One was able to learn so much about the patient, the family and the conditions in which they lived, and it was a great privilege to be greeted and ushered up to someone's bedroom, even if they were a stranger to you. Alas, such visits are rare today. They do not feature among the boxes that have to be ticked to satisfy the authorities. Even less frequent, I am told, are the occasions when the GP seeks the aid of a consultant on a "domiciliary visit". They were able to see the patient together at his home where the GP received the benefit of the consultant's specialised knowledge at the bedside.

When I left general practice I was privileged to be appointed the medical director of a newly built hospice. It was here that I found what I can only honestly describe as "old fashioned medical care" still practised. The staff were free from bureaucratic regulations and were able to exercise what in their professional judgment was in the best interest of their patients. Furthermore, they were not concerned so much with modern diagnostic techniques as relieving suffering. It must be acknowledged that this palliative relief of unpleasant symptoms lay in the hands of the nurses rather than the doctors. Compassion, gentle physical contact, listening and giving time were all attributes of the good hospice nurse, and not delivered on a prescription pad. She was more concerned that there was no wrinkle in the bottom sheet causing soreness than monitoring a machine administering an intra-venous drip. The Greeks had a word for this particular love and concern for the welfare of their fellow men: αγαπε (agape). One cannot help wondering whether the opportunity to exercise these gifts made so many excellent nurses wish to leave the wards of the general hospital and work at the hospice instead.

It's a brave man these days who runs a practice single handed. Most GPs are in a group practice of three, four or more doctors. Consequently one does not often have one's own doctor. Although assigned to a particular doctor you are likely to see any doctor in the group who is available. You may have to wait several days to get an appointment with the doctor of your choice. If you need to be seen urgently for medical or social reasons you will be seen by the doctor who is available or "on call". This is a perfectly reasonable policy, but it has completely eroded the concept of a Family Doctor, a role which was disappearing even fifty years ago. It used to be the case that one doctor looked after two or three, or even four, generations of the same family. I myself was only deprived of attending a member of the fifth generation of the same family owing to the daughter in the fourth having a miscarriage shortly before I retired. The Family Doctor did more than attend to their various ills; he fulfilled an almost pastoral role, being regarded as Guide, Philosopher and Friend, rather than as a purveyor of NHS services.

In the 1930s a firm called May and Baker produced a drug called 'M and B 693'. It was the first drug effective in killing bacteria and really the predecessor of all antibiotics. For the first time doctors had at their disposal an agent which acted on scientific principles to cure infections and it, and its successors, demolished a hundred nostrums. But the scientific approach also removed the mysticism which hitherto the medical profession had used as a cloak for their therapeutic incompetence. Once mysticism has been removed then awe and wonder also disappear and, it must be said, some respect. Once the doctor is regarded as a skilful technician, much as the television engineer, and not as someone possessing mysterious knowledge, then his opinion is open to questioning and testing, and now the internet is available to all there is no impediment to a searching enquiry as to the validity of his opinion.

Without wishing to appear presumptuous, an analogy can be drawn between the ways in which the attitude to the medical profession has changed with that to the royal family. Before the war the sovereign was seen rarely except in grainy news films on the way to opening parliament or some such event, or on the face of postage stamps. Mysticism was preserved and with it a loyal reverence. Criticism was almost treasonable. Now the magic has been removed by television and the Royals are exposed as mortals such as us, and with this unveiling they are exposed to criticism which would not have been tolerated previously.

The following tales record incidents which might have occurred to any of my contemporaries. They reflect the varied and colourful nature of the work of a GP. I hope that my successors will be able to enjoy similar experiences.

Shot in Whitehall

When I was a medical student I lived in lodgings just north of St. Johns Wood. To return home from the hospital I used to catch a bus (a number 159 I remember) from Whitehall.

One rather wet and blustery winter's evening, while waiting at the bus stop, I saw a gentleman descending the steps of the treasury, clad in homberg and a black overcoat, briefcase in hand, suddenly collapse and cry out. A crowd gathered round. For the first and last time in my life, I said, "Let me through, I'm a doctor."

This certainly wasn't true as I had not yet sat my qualifying exams, but it sounded good, and I was in no mood for niceties!

"I think I've been shot," the prostrate figure announced. This sounded unlikely, and produced gasps of horror from the crowd.

"Here, in my knee," he said. Kneeling down on the pavement I rolled up the pin striped trouser leg, and there, sure enough, was a small round puncture hole on the inside of his left knee joint. Furthermore, when I felt his knee I could detect a foreign body, about one and a half inches long, lying under the skin.

The situation was becoming more complicated than I had at first anticipated, and I was beginning to regret my eagerness to assert my professional status. I humm-ed and hah-ed for a bit and then acted sensibly, if belatedly, by calling an ambulance. When it arrived I directed it to the casualty department of St. Thomas's hospital across the river, and assured the victim I would enquire after him tomorrow.

First thing next morning I made enquiries of the formidable lady known as "Sister Casualty."

"Oh! It was you, was it? Silly young man. Shot indeed! It was a pencil."

The civil servant had placed an ordinary, lead pencil in the right hand pocket of his long black overcoat. Unfortunately there was a hole in this pocket through which the pencil had slipped, and had fallen between the layers of the coat to the bottom hem. When running down the steps of the treasury, his advancing right knee had struck the rear end of the pencil, forcing the sharp point through his overcoat and trousers into the flesh over his left knee, and had then snapped off, leaving the broken portion of the pencil under the skin, and the remainder still inside his overcoat lining.

Some weeks later I was reading the British Medical Journal and came across a letter from a G.P. describing how a patient of his, while walking in the woods, had suddenly experienced a sharp pain in his knee. Looking down he saw the pointed end of a pencil protruding from the skin. He had no idea how the pencil had got there but suggested that, as it was of just the right calibre, it had been fired from a small rifle by some irresponsible youth.

I knew better!

I immediately wrote to the doctor suggesting that if he were to search in the bottom hem of the coat or Macintosh which his patient had been wearing at the time of the supposed attack, I was confident that he would find the other portion of pencil.

I posted my letter fully expecting an answer congratulating me on my Holmes-like powers of deduction and acknowledging my startling acumen.

I never heard a word.

My First Patient

Having studied for six years to achieve one specific goal, passed numerous examinations and eventually found oneself entitled to be addressed as "Doctor", it is perhaps not surprising that the accomplishment is accompanied by an exaggerated estimation of one's capabilities. A newly qualified doctor can be a danger to his patients if he is not aware that his knowledge, although extensive, has yet to be enhanced and matured by experience.

It used to be the custom that, if one was lucky enough to be employed by the hospital which had trained you, and the competition for such jobs was very keen, the first job offered to the newly qualified doctor would be that of casualty officer.

The casualty department, open twenty four hours a day and seven days a week, attracted every sort of illness and many varieties of patient to its doors. During one shift on duty one might see a child with earache, individuals with broken bones, heart attacks, acute abdominal pain, drunks, street accidents and vagrants in search of warmth and a cup of tea.

Supervising the department, and creating order out of seeming chaos, was "Sister Casualty." It was her job to sort out the trivia from those seriously ill, and, more importantly, to marshal the casualty officers, "My Young Men" as she called them, into some kind of team that could deal effectively with the crowd of yelling children, the rows of patients sitting on benches waiting their turn, the seriously ill lying on stretchers or in cubicles, and the importunate clamourers who found themselves in the wrong department. It was to this department, as a Casualty Officer clad in a short white jacket, (long white coats were worn by the more senior doctors), that I started medical practice and came face to face with my first patient as a qualified doctor.

Seated at a small table with the necessary forms in front of me, I started to question a plump little old lady who had asked to see a doctor on a matter of some urgency.

"Good morning. May I have your name?"

"Doris Vincent," she replied. Even today confidentiality prevents me from divulging her real name: one I have never forgotten.

"And your age?"

"Eighty four."

"And what is it that you are complaining of?" I asked, in the manner I had been taught.

"Oh! I'm not complaining, doctor. I'm pregnant by the Holy Ghost."

The training that I had received in all branches of medicine over the past six years had been both of a high quality and very extensive, but nothing that I could recall from my student days had equipped me to deal with this particular set of circumstances.

Desperately stalling for time I asked, "Have you any idea as to the date of conception?"

"Pentecost, doctor." the answer came back like a rifle shot.

This completely floored me, as apart from other considerations, which made the situation a trifle difficult for me to handle, I had no idea when Pentecost was.

At this stage I wisely decided that the acquiring of a medical degree did not impart omniscience to the holder, and that I was out of my depth.

I referred Doris Vincent to higher authority, and it was with some sense of failure that I later saw her handed over to the psychiatrists.

My Last Patient

The post of a casualty officer lasted six months. At the end of that period I had become accustomed to coping, more or less adequately, with the lesser ills of the flesh which presented themselves in a thousand different forms at the doors of the hospital. In truth, I had perhaps become a little blasé, and was anxious to start on my next job, which would be on the wards.

It was inevitable that, though the department never closed, there were times when a casualty officer was not immediately available. On such an occasion he could be summoned by a bell which rang throughout the hospital. To each doctor was ascribed a particular combination of "tings" on the bell, so that each could identify his own particular call. In the case of an emergency this call was immediately repeated: a process known as "double ringing," which indicated that the doctor's presence was required immediately.

It was a Sunday morning, my last day on duty as a casualty officer. I was trying to raise some enthusiasm for a cold and greasy sausage and egg on my plate in the residents' dining room, when I heard my series of "tings" on the bell, and then immediately again. Having become, as I said, accustomed to various emergencies over the preceding six months, I finished the sausage before reporting to Sister to enquire the cause of the alarm.

Sister had been in charge of casualty for many years, and there were not many situations which she could not size up with a shrewd glance and a few well directed questions. She knew, and we knew she knew, far more about the running of the department and the treatment of the patients than we, as newly qualified doctors, could hope to. Nevertheless on certain occasions she tended to become very excited. Her agitation sometimes arose from the nature of the accident for which she was trying to provide help, but more often, it must be confessed, it was due to one of her "young men" committing an act which she considered stupid, or not in the patient's best interests. On such occasions she would become a little suffused in the face, but the tell-tale sign that presaged a dire emergency or serious trouble for some luckless casualty officer, was the movement of her behind. It would wag like the tail of an Aylesbury duck on its way to water. On this occasion her behind was sending out alarm signals like a Geiger counter confronting a block of uranium.

"There's a man in that cubicle who looks very ill and is behaving rather oddly. I'd like you to see him at once."

Obediently I entered the cubicle to find a man in his fifties, lying on the couch clasping his stomach and groaning. I asked him what appeared to be the matter.

"I've got an obstruction, doctor."

Vaguely annoyed at being given a diagnosis rather than a complaint, I said, "What sort of obstruction and where is it?"

"I've got a bottle up my backside, doctor, and I can feel it 'ere," he said, placing his hand just below his chest.

"Sister must be having one of her off days," I thought, "This man is obviously barmy."

To humour him I lay him on his back, extracted him from his trousers and laid a hand on his abdomen. To my amazement I felt a hard lump in the upper part of his abdomen, below his ribs, where he had placed his hand. The matter obviously merited further investigation. I asked him to turn onto his left side, and, having donned a rubber glove, I cautiously inserted my finger into his rectum. Almost immediately the examining finger encountered another hard object, which it was not difficult to identify as being made of glass. A moment later it was apparent that it was the bottom of a bottle, and, furthermore, a wine bottle, as I could feel the indented punt. The lump I had first felt in the upper portion of his abdomen had to be the neck of the same bottle.

More than a little amazed I stood back.

"You are quite right, I said, "You have got a bottle up your backside."

And then, although it was no business of mine, I could not resist asking: "Do you mind telling me how it got there?"

"I was out with a woman last night," he said, and then added ruefully, "Some people do do the most damn stupid things."

One felt he had a point.

When a casualty officer encountered a problem beyond his clinical competence, he was obliged to write the full details of the case on the patient's notes, and then hand them to a porter whose job it was to find the resident assistant surgeon or physician. They were the two most senior members of the junior staff and as such were not summoned by bells. By the time the porter had found his quarry, who might be anywhere in a very large hospital, and he in turn had read the notes, given them his consideration, finished what he was engaged upon at the time and then made his way to casualty, an hour or more might have elapsed between his being summoned and his arrival.

On this occasion, instead of writing; "Possible appendicitis. Will R.A.S. please see?" or something similar, I wrote: "Wine bottle in rectum. Will R.A.S. please advise further action?"

I handed the notes to the porter and sat down to await events. Hardly had I settled into my seat when the surgeon appeared, notes in hand and eyebrows up to his hair line.

"Where is this man?" he demanded.

It was a Sunday morning, when consultants did not usually grace the hospital precincts. There were plenty of well-trained assistant staff well able to cope with all but the most serious problems. It was therefore with some surprise that when I followed my patient to the operating theatre that afternoon, I found that performing the operation were two consultant surgeons, assisted by the resident surgeon and a consultant anaesthetist. So efficiently had the hospital grapevine relayed the news that the whole of the gallery, used by students to watch operations, was filled with off-duty nurses.

The bottle was delivered by a pair of midwifery forceps held by one consultant, the other assisting its downwards passage by pressure from above.

They never found the cork and they never found the label, but the bottle has a place in the hospital museum to this day.

Boanerges

I don't know why I called him (he was undoubtedly male) Boanerges. He certainly had no biblical connections, and although he made a distinctive noise it bore no relation to thunder. He was my first car: a twenty four year old 1929 Morris Cowley coupe.

The coupe bit was an affectation; the driving and passenger seats were enclosed in a cabin while the rear two seats were open to the air in the form of a bench with a back that shut down when not in use. This alfresco arrangement was known as a dicky.

Having nothing so sophisticated as a petrol pump the carburettor was supplied by gravity feed from the tank which was situated under the bonnet just in front of the windscreen. Apart from giving a modern health and safety official nightmares this ensured that the driver was surrounded by a miasma of petrol fumes. I soon gave up smoking as it was certainly not safe to smoke anywhere near the vehicle and I found I could not afford to run a car as well as buy cigarettes.

When I had a weekend off duty I went home to my parents down the old Great West Road. Returning on one occasion I was stopped in Kensington Gore by two traffic cops on motor cycles. They were known as Triumph Twins as they hunted in pairs on maroon Triumph machines. "We have stopped you sir, because of the general condition of your vehicle. Your exhaust is broken, your steering seems defective and your left rear wing is falling off." To my great embarrassment they then proceeded to peer into Boanerges' viscera and lie underneath to assess the condition of his transmission, brakes and cables while I stood by as an anxious spectator surrounded by the roar of London's traffic. Presence of mind is not usually one of my assets, but as the larger and senior officer approached me, notebook open and pencil threateningly poised, it suddenly occurred to me that St. Thomas's was the hospital for all the metropolitan police.

"Thank you," I said, "for giving my car such a thorough inspection. I hope I would do the same for you should you ever have to come to St. Thomas's hospital." His manner immediately changed from being official and menacing to friendly and conciliatory.

"As a matter of fact, sir, I recently had my appendix out at St. Thomas's: lovely nurses there."

The notebook snapped shut; the pencil was replaced behind his ear, "Don't you ever let me catch you out in this rattle-trap again," he said as he remounted his Triumph.

The news of my engagement filtered up through the hospital hierarchy until it reached the ears of my chief, a consultant physician. "Congratulations, my boy," he said one morning before the ward round. "You must bring the girl to dinner."

Sometime later I received an invitation, via his secretary, to take my fiancée to dinner in his flat above his consulting rooms.

With some trepidation we set off for Harley Street and parked Boanerges next to a Bentley. Introductions were made. "Where's the ring, eh? Why no ring?" he asked me.

"I'm sorry, sir, I can't afford to buy a ring until I've sold my car."

"Car?" he said, "What car?"

"It's parked just outside, sir."

He went over to the window and, drawing back the heavy curtains, peered out.

"What do you want for it?" he asked.

"I was hoping to get £50," I replied.

"I will give you £50 for it now if you promise never to park it outside my rooms ever again," he said.

He was as good as his word. My future wife and I returned to the hospital by bus with a cheque in my pocket.

The ring only cost £45, but I did not think it necessary to tell him that.

An Officer and a Gentleman

During the war a medical student was in a reserved occupation. The government realised that, unless the flow of newly qualified doctors was maintained throughout the war, the inevitable lack of doctors, both to serve in the armed forces and afterwards in peace-time civilian practice, would be a severe problem. Once qualified one was called up for active service or, when hostilities ceased, for the prescribed period of National Service. Further dispensation could be obtained for a short period to gain experience from junior hospital appointments, but sooner or later the demands of military service had to be met.

So it was that I found myself in the company of a dozen other young doctors at an R.A.F. station in Lytham St. Annes, where it was the task of the regular officers and N.C.O.s to teach us how to become officers and gentlemen. It soon became apparent that the triple role of officer, gentleman and doctor was going to prove too heavy a burden for me to bear. I think one has to be blessed with a certain temperament to find military life appealing. To so many brilliant people it has been the medium in which their talents have flourished. To others, the ritual, the uniform, the rank consciousness, the enforced camaraderie of mess life and the contrived formalities of special occasions, give an impression of unreality. It did not take long for me, and my superiors, to become aware that my future career, if it were to flourish, would not be in uniform.

I was posted to an R.A.F. hospital as a "u/t Med. Spec." The "u/t" meant that I was either "untrained," or "under training." I never discovered which.

The Commanding Officer of the hospital was a Group Captain. He was also a doctor, but had not had a stethoscope in his ears for the past thirty years. Administration was his strong suit, and in his spare time he could give an expert opinion on old railway lines and Roman roads in Britain.

Shortly after my arrival I was walking across the parade ground in front of the hospital dressed in my "Number Ones," when I noticed two attractive officers of the Princess Mary's R.A.F. Nursing Service approaching me. Being a well brought up young man I took my hat off to them as they passed. The result was not as I had expected. The window of the adjutant's office, which looked out on to the parade ground, shot up with a bang.

"That officer there, come here immediately."

I was left in no doubt that I had offended the Service, the unit, my commission and Her Majesty, and also, and most particularly, the adjutant.

My responsibility was a ward of newly recruited airmen. They had been assembled from all parts of the country, had been accommodated in close proximity, for the most part in damp Nissen huts, and had undertaken hard physical training. The predictable result was that they succumbed to every known complication of the common cold, cough and sore throat: sinusitis, pneumonia, acute rheumatic fever, acute nephritis, and others. I was supervised by a regular officer, who also looked after the officers' ward.

Each month the Commanding Officer performed an inspection of my ward. Sufficient notice was given of this event to enable the floor to be scrubbed, the sheets changed, the beds aligned and the patients warned to behave in a suitably respectful and deferential manner. He was accompanied by the matron, a formidable lady covered in red tabs, whom I never saw on any other occasion, the adjutant and the catering officer, (to ensure that no airman would be ill-advised enough to complain about the food). They processed round the ward in single file with myself bringing the rear. Questions were occasionally asked about an airman's illness, but as the C.O.'s clinical knowledge was strictly limited these were not pursued, about the food, and occasionally about their home or family. Having completed the circuit of the ward the cortège marched off, helped on their way by a smartish salute from the "u/t Med. Spec."

On one occasion the C.O. took it into his head to examine the lavatories: the usual row of urinals and cubicles at the end of the ward. Marching in, he pushed open the door of the first cubicle with his swagger stick.

"There's no paper in here," he barked.

"Coming over, chum," said a voice from the neighbouring closet, and a roll of paper landed at his feet. For some reason, which I could never understand, the adjutant held me responsible for this embarrassing incident.

Shortly before I had completed my appointed period of National Service I was sent for by the C.O.: an unprecedented occurrence.

"Tell me, Jones," he said, "Are you thinking of applying for a Permanent Commission in the Service?"

After a respectful pause, which I hoped would give the impression that I was giving the question my serious consideration, I replied,

"No, sir. I think probably not."

"Can't help feeling you're right, Jones," he said. "Although you've been in the Service I've never really thought of you as being of the Service."

At last the C.O. and I had found something about which we were in entire agreement.

Never Say "Never"

"Appendicitis never occurs before the age of two years." I can see the elderly consultant delivering himself of this opinion now, surrounded by a crowd of students, including myself.

I had only joined the practice three weeks previously, and was very much on probation, both from my partners and my patients, when I was summoned to see a baby of eighteen months, with abdominal pain, diarrhoea and vomiting. I had no hesitation in diagnosing an attack of gastroenteritis. When I was asked to call again next day the child's condition was worse. He was screaming and impossible to examine. I was a bit worried and promised to call again later. When I did call again that evening I found that the child had ceased to vomit or have diarrhoea, but was obviously very ill, and, most ominously, his abdomen felt hard. I sent him into hospital accompanied by two very worried parents.

Next morning I rang the hospital for news. The child had been operated on for generalised peritonitis due to a ruptured appendix.

There followed three of the most anxious days of my life. I visited the ward as often as work permitted, to be confronted by two rightfully angry parents sitting by their critically ill child.

It was only due to skilful surgery and nursing that the patient survived, and I was spared a nightmare which would have haunted me for the rest of my career. Quite understandably that family ceased to be patients of our practice, and I did not see them again.

Some twenty years later I was carrying out pre-employment medical examinations for a local firm.

"What's that nasty scar on your stomach?" I asked a burly bearded youth lying on the examination couch.

"Had my appendix out when I was a baby. My mum says I nearly died 'cos the doctor didn't diagnose it."

I looked at the name on his notes. It was one I had never forgotten. I kept very quiet.

Blood Money

She had a strong sense of civic duty: a retired secretary who quietly did a lot of good, without being a do-gooder. One service she considered to be an inescapable obligation was to give blood; but she hated doing it.

"I know it's silly of me, doctor, but I detest the whole process. I can't stand needles, the sight of blood makes me feel ill, and the smell of it makes me nauseated when I go to the clinic."

Nothing would stop her giving her pint however, and whenever asked to attend, she would grit her teeth, summon up her courage and take the bus into the city to do her duty.

"They tell me that I have a special blood group, so my blood is badly needed," she said, and indeed she was of the group that made her blood compatible with that of all other groups: a universal donor.

She developed arthritis of the hip and experienced increasing pain from it. Serial X-rays showed progressive destruction of the joint. She was in urgent need of a hip replacement and was placed on the waiting list. Despite analgesics her pain increased and prevented sleep. When I tried to hasten her admission I was told that it would be "at least another eighteen months."

Eventually she could put up with it no longer.

"I feel very guilty, doctor, but I have decided to have it done privately. I can't afford it myself, but my nephew has very kindly offered to lend me some money. Of course I will have to pay him back."

Two weeks later, her hip was replaced. She was overjoyed. She was able to walk without pain and, above all, to enjoy an uninterrupted night's sleep.

"They were very kind to me at the hospital, doctor. Nothing was too much trouble for them. There was just one thing…" She started searching in her handbag. "I'm not complaining of course, but…" and she retrieved a sheet of paper which she handed to me. "At the bottom, doctor," she said.

It was the bill from the hospital. After entries for occupancy of hospital bed, operating theatre fee, cost of prosthesis and drugs, the last entry read:

"Two pints of blood at £20 each: £40."

Checkmate

He was obviously a stubborn man. Even now, he had agreed to see me only because his wife had insisted. I could not remember attending him before and had some difficulty in finding the house. He was sitting up in bed surrounded by books and papers, belittling his illness, apologising for troubling me and berating his wife for asking me to call. I had plenty of time to glance round the room and at the books lying on his bed. Seeing one entitled *The Acol System* I remarked that though I played bridge I could not cope with anything so sophisticated in the way of bidding conventions.

"Oh! What system do you play then?" he asked.

Rather sheepishly I replied, "Just simple stuff. Culbertson basically, I suppose."

"Ah yes, good old kitchen Culbertson. You should grow up and try Acol when you've more time. You'll find it makes a much better game."

Getting a little tired of his supercilious attitude to my modest bridge playing techniques, I produced a thermometer and placed it in his mouth, effectively preventing further patronising remarks. During the ensuing silence I spotted a *Daily Telegraph* lying on the sheets beside him, with the crossword half finished. Seeing a chance to re-establish my position I said:

"Well, I may not play Acol, but at least I aspire to doing the *Times'* crossword, rather than *The Telegraph's.*"

"Really," he said, removing the thermometer from his mouth. "That's very interesting. I used to make them up."

Coffee

Night calls are never welcome. Most of them are bred of anxiety rather than medical necessity. The pain nagging for a week, becomes intolerable at 2.00a.m.; the child's cough, which has kept him off school for the last two days, seems more persistent and the patient more fractious: "Perhaps it's pneumonia; better be safe and call the doctor." These are understandable causes for alarm, but the doctor at the other end of the telephone can nearly always detect which request for a visit will merely need reassurance, and which will require urgent treatment.

"My husband has got a severe pain in his chest. He says it's indigestion, but he's sweating and looks awful." Such a message will get any G.P. out of bed and reaching for his trousers in double quick time. When I had been in practice about two years I received a call in the middle of one night from a lady in the village along these lines:

"I'm sorry to call you, doctor. I'm not a patient of yours, but I live near you. My brother is visiting me from Kenya, and he has woken up and can't get his breath. It's

40

like asthma. He's sitting on the edge of his bed gasping for air."

One does not need to have had a great deal of medical experience to know that what was being described was a form of heart attack. The heart muscle is failing to pump blood through the lungs which are getting increasingly congested, and the distressed patient is in effect drowning in his own blood. Such an attack very commonly occurs at night. Fortunately I was able to treat this patient successfully. He made a good recovery and was very grateful.

Two or three weeks later he said to me, "I have only one wish, and that is to get back to my coffee farm outside Nairobi before I die. I want you to come with me to see that I do. I will provide you with a first class return ticket and pay a reasonable fee."

Here was the offer of an experience not made to many young G.P.s. I approached my senior partner at that time. He was a man who even the most charitable would not have described as being of the most generous or considerate disposition, and certainly not to junior partners. He was obviously envious of my being offered such an opportunity, and reluctant to let me go. However, I think the prospect of a fat fee, of which he would be entitled to the lion's share, persuaded him, "But," he insisted, "You must return immediately."

I am speaking of a time before commercial jet travel. We were driven to Heathrow by taxi and boarded an aircraft which, as I recall, was called an Argonaut. Instead of jetting along at 30,000 ft. and 500 miles an hour arriving at Nairobi eight hours later, our progress, forty years ago, was a little more arduous. The four-engined aircraft was slow, noisy and thirsty. The four propellers beat their way laboriously through the air to Rome, thence to Benghazi in Libya, on to Khartoum, then Entebbe and finally across Lake Victoria to Nairobi, resting at each stop while the aircraft was serviced and refuelled, and taking twenty four hours to accomplish the journey.

I had never been to Africa before, and I was fascinated by the drive from the airport, past the African villages and through the bush, to Kiambu, where his farm lay. Arriving at the house my patient immediately made for the verandah and called for a drink. My eyes popped out of my head when I saw him pour out a very generous measure of Remy Martin, and then fill the glass up to the top with soda.

Any man who could afford to drown the best liqueur brandy with such nonchalance must be very rich, I thought. Looking southwards over the Nairobi plain from the verandah one could just see in the far blue distance the outline of Kilimanjaro, with its snow-capped peak: a sight I have never forgotten.

My impression of my patient's wealth was confirmed next morning when his son-in-law took me round the farm. The rows and rows of bushes bearing beans making some of the best coffee in the world yielded, he told me, about a thousand tons at £100 a ton, (or was it a hundred tons at £1000 a ton?). I was beginning to understand about the brandy, and was wondering if it was too late to revise my fee. The trip was a brief interlude of magic from another world, but nevertheless it was with great pleasure that I returned home to my wife and family on a bleak November day, forty-eight hours later.

I kept in touch with my patient. He suffered a stroke a year or so later, but by diligent application and conscientious practice he recovered the use of his right arm sufficiently to be able to raise a glass of brandy and soda to his lips at regular intervals.

Jessie

They were a quaint old couple: two spinsters who lived in an unenviable council house on the outskirts of the city, long since pulled down and replaced by a row of neat, comfortable looking bungalows. I climbed upstairs to see Miss Sparrow, coughing and wheezing in the double bed, the window closed, but still admitting a blast of air from the North East. Missing the warmth of her companion in the other half of the bed, she had a shawl round her shoulders and a hot water bottle, now luke-warm, under the heavy quilts. I remonstrated with her gently about the temperature of the room, but I suspected there was little they could do to warm it.

Going downstairs again, taking care not to catch my shoe in the frayed carpet, I sat in front of a blazing fire in the front room, and prepared to write a prescription for something to ease her cough. It was many years ago, and perhaps I was more conscientious in those days in following the health authority's injunction to enter the full name of the patient at the top of the form. In any event I asked her companion what her name was.

"Sparrow, doctor."

"Yes, I know that, but what's her Christian name?"

"Her Christian name?"

"Yes."

She looked puzzled, shuffled to the door and opened it.

"Jessie," she caterwauled up the stairs, "what's your Christian name?"

Mary and Mrs. Gray

Five maids and three gardeners in one household might seem a little excessive these days, but between the wars any wealthy family living in a large country house might well have found the need to employ as many staff. Such a style of living denoted wealth, and leisure to enjoy it. The London season with it dinners and balls, Royal Ascot, Wimbledon and Henley, culminating in Glorious Goodwood and Cowes Week: these were the pastimes of the "idle rich"; and then there was salmon fishing to be had in Scotland or Norway if boredom set in. Such pleasures must have brought happiness to many, but Mrs. Gray was not a happy lady.

Mr. Gray had been in the Royal Navy, but was of independent means and when asked his occupation could well have answered: "Gentleman." Having lost his first wife some years previously he married the daughter of his neighbours, a lady some twenty years younger than himself. It was not a happy marriage. They had no children and lived in the large house attended by the eight members of staff until, in 1941, Mr. Gray died. His will was curious. He left the house and all his estate to the daughter of his first marriage, a lady who lived in

America. His widow was left nothing, other than a modest allowance paid to her each month by the bank, who was his trustee. Mrs. Gray soon found that her allowance was insufficient to enable her to pay the expenses of the house. Fortunately, perhaps, the maids and gardeners were called up for war service. Consequently in 1942 Mrs. Gray found herself living alone in this imposing house which she was unable to maintain.

It was at this time that she was joined by Mary, aged 14, a girl who had lived all her life in the neighbouring village and was seeking a position in domestic service. She was engaged by Mrs. Gray for 12/6d a week and worked from 7.00a.m. to 10.00p.m. every day, with one half day off a week. Together Mary and Mrs. Gray set about creating two flats in the house, which were let out to augment Mrs. Gray's income. Then, in 1943, the house was requisitioned by the navy, and Mrs. Gray and her tenants were given two weeks to get out.

She found herself with no house, no friends and a small income, and she now began to be afflicted by increasing deafness. She did have one faithful friend, Mary, who offered to take her under her own roof and so the lady of the house came to live with her parlour maid, now aged 16, and her elderly mother, in their modest cottage in the village. And there she stayed for six months.

Eventually she was able to rent furnished accommodation in a nearby village, and Mary, her wages now raised to £1 a week, moved in with her to look after her. Mrs. Gray had no cooking or housekeeping skills and her deafness was causing her to become increasingly isolated. This arrangement continued for two years until, in 1946, with £2,000 left her by her estranged mother, Mrs. Gray bought a small, rather ugly, house in 1/4 acre of garden. It was within bicycling distance of Mary's cottage who continued to look after her.

By now, Mary was being courted by William, whom she had known since she was 14. William had been demobilised from the RAF. and had been apprenticed to a boat building firm, and was later employed by a builder. In 1954 Mary and William were married and moved into the cottage with Mary's mother. William had always wanted to be a teacher, and two years after his marriage Mrs. Gray increased Mary's wages to £4 a week. This enabled her to support William while he was at the teachers' training college, for which he received no grant and, of course, no payment.

Meanwhile Mary spent nearly all day, every day, looking after Mrs. Gray in her house. There were no callers, no friends and no visitors and her deafness was now impenetrable. As if this was not enough, in 1956 it became apparent that Mrs. Gray was ill. She was later found to have a form of cancer of the bone marrow, for which at that time there was no effective treatment. I remember going to see her shortly before Christmas. I had driven from our house leaving my wife, our two year old daughter and baby son in warmth and comfort surrounded with decorations and so many Christmas cards that we had difficulty in knowing where to put them. I found Mrs. Gray sitting in a chair in her sitting room huddled over the fire. On the mantelpiece sat one Christmas card: the only one she had received. It was from her bank manager.

The last stages of her illness were distressing, more for Mary, faithfully trying to keep her comfortable, than for Mrs. Gray herself. The cancer had affected other organs, and she died, in January 1958, aged 70, after delirium, convulsions and coma caused by kidney failure. Mary made all the funeral arrangements and she and Mrs Gray's daily help were the only mourners, as the bank manager could not come.

Mrs. Gray's will was very simple. She left everything to Mary, but had added a small unofficial codicil: "Please look after my bank manager and my doctor."

Mary, William and Mary's mother left their cottage in the village and moved into Mrs. Gray's house. William had completed his training and was teaching wood and metalcraft at a local school. Their first child, a son, was born in 1955. He was delivered at home by Mary's great friend, the distrct nurse. In those days the district nurses were midwives, health visitors, social workers, and many other things. Nothing went on in her village that the district nurse did not know about. She knew why Betty Baker was suffering from morning sickness before Betty Baker did. The district nurse who delivered Mary's son was called Georgina, and, in recognition of her friendship and service, Mary and William named their son George.

George grew up, did well at school and decided that he wanted to be a doctor. Needing some useful experience with which to impress those who were to interview him for a place at medical school, Mary asked for my help. I approached a friend, who was the pathologist in the local hospital, and he gave him an unpaid position in his laboratory, where he showed great promise. He was accepted by a London teaching hospital, duly qualified and decided to be an anaesthetist.

He did well achieving his Diploma in Anaesthetics. Then one day he rang up his parents to tell them that he was giving it all up and leaving medicine.

"I am on duty from Friday morning until Monday evening, day and night and get very little sleep or rest. I feel exhausted. I cannot do my job properly and one day, if I go on like this, I am going to kill someone, so I am stopping before that happens."

This story has a happy ending. George went on to teach, like his father, and then in the autumn of 2002 he again rang his parents, this time to say "I'm going back into medicine again." He is now much happier, and well on his way to becoming a consultant anaesthetist.

Mary, now aged 75 and William, had two more children, sold the house Mrs. Gray had left them, and now live in a bungalow of their own, not far away.

Neither Christian nor Scientific

Christian scientists make the most satisfactory patients. They never call one or ask for advice until natural processes have been given every chance, and when they do call you, you know that there is something seriously wrong, and that it is nothing trivial.

A very rich family lived in a large house on the hill. They were well known to be militant Christian scientists, so none of us was ever called to attend them – until one night.

My senior partner was on call that night for night calls, and very thankful I was too, as it was a pig of a winter's night. It had snowed hard, thawed, and then frozen again. The roads were sheets of ice, with snow banks on each side. The telephone rang:

"This is the butler at Mr. Bloggs' house. I am sorry to worry you doctor, but I am very worried about Mr. Bloggs. He has been in bed for a few days with a nasty cough, and now he is burning hot and rambling in his mind. I know he don't like doctors, but he's all alone here, the family is away and I really am very worried, doctor. Do you think you could come?"

My partner took the call and realised that whatever the difficulties he would have to go. Doubtless he put on the conventional gear for night visits: trousers over pyjama trousers with socks tucked in, sweater over pyjama jacket, and an extra layer or two for warmth.

The house stood on a hill up some fairly narrow lanes, and while negotiating a bend the inevitable happened. His car skidded into a ditch up to the axles in snow. It was the middle of the night in a lonely road, help was not to hand and the house was still some way off. There was nothing for it. He abandoned his car and set off on foot along the icy road, carrying his doctor's bag.

Some time later he arrived at the house to be met by the butler. "He seems much better now, sir. I didn't dare tell him I'd sent for you."

My partner wearily climbed the stairs to the bedroom and introduced himself. Alas, during the hours intervening since the original cry for help, the crisis had passed, the fever had subsided, delirium resolved and rational thought restored.

"What the devil are you doing here? I do not want a doctor. See yourself out."

The walk back to the car must have seemed a long way.

Renal Colic

It does a doctor no harm to experience a few ills and pains himself. To be the other end of the stethoscope is a humiliating but valuable experience in helping him to appreciate what his patients are actually feeling when they are trying to describe their symptoms to him.

Many years ago when our children were still very young we were unwise enough to take the advice of a travel agent, and we embarked on a package holiday to a beach resort in Majorca. It is no part of this story to describe the collation of horrors which this event produced, but among the many other features which failed to measure up to the delights enumerated in the glossy brochure, were the hotel beds. They were of a particularly sadistic continental design, and every morning I woke up with a back-ache which was not relieved until I had been vertical for an hour or more.

One morning the back-ache was more persistent than usual, and after breakfast, instead of slowly improving, as it had previously, it appeared to be increasing in intensity. I decided to forego the pleasure of lying on the beach in the close company of two thousand of my countrymen, and, sending the family off with rubber rings and bathing suits, I returned to the rack of my bed.

An hour or so later, the pain having in no way diminished, I found myself making frequent trips to the primitive lavatory supplied by the management, to pass water, vomit or both. Slowly, slowly the truth dawned; the penny dropped: I was having an attack of renal colic.

Of all the pains mortal flesh is heir to, it is generally agreed that that which is experienced when trying to pass a stone down the tube which leads from the kidney to the bladder is among the most fearsome. Women who have given birth to ten pound babies, and have also experienced a severe attack of renal colic, unhesitatingly state their preference for producing the baby rather than the stone.

My faith in my continental colleagues is not unshakeable. It may therefore be taken as a measure of my extreme distress, that by mid-morning I had knocked up the couple in the next door compartment, (she, I remember, had recently had a hysterectomy and had come on the same holiday in the mistaken belief that she would enjoy a quiet period of convalescence), and asked them to send for a Spanish doctor. Meanwhile I sweated, groaned, urinated and vomited. I was quite determined that on the arrival of my medical attendant it was going to be I that made both the diagnosis and prescribed the treatment. So when, some two hours later, el medico appeared, I was able by various gestures to convey the nature of my troubles to him, and suggested that an injection of Pethidine, a strong pain killer, might be appropriate.

"Penicillin?" he asked.

"No, Peth-id-ine."

No sign of recognition or comprehension appeared on his smiling face. Obviously Pethidine was not marketed in the Balearics.

A little mystified he shuffled off and returned a few minutes later with what appeared to be a precursor of a modern Primus stove. This he took into our bathroom and with its help proceeded to sterilise a large syringe. His aseptic technique would have filled me with greater confidence had not our loo, in the best tradition of continental models, leaked on to the floor.

Having completed his preparations to his satisfaction he reappeared with his very large syringe loaded with a murky fluid. By a series of picturesque gestures, accompanied by a flow of Spanish, he indicated that he intended to thrust it into my backside. As I rolled over to expose my buttocks I managed to ask him the nature of the concoction I was about to receive. On hearing his reply, I had for a moment a vivid recollection of an advertisement I had recently received for this particular drug on the back of a piece of blotting paper.

"Particularly recommended for the treatment of women suffering from painful periods," had been its caption.

I was in no position to argue.

"And if no good," he said, "Morphium. But now," he added as a Parthian shot, whipping a prescription pad out of his breast pocket, "Suppositore."

And he departed.

"Hullo, Daddy," said our youngest, returning from the beach, "How's the back?" I had to confess to my incredulous wife the resorts I had been forced to in their absence, adding that she had better get the "Suppositores" as I was not much in favour of the "Morphium."

Still a little startled and worried at the turn of events, she went off in search of a Pharmacia. She returned some three-quarters of an hour later, hot and frustrated.

"Did you get them?" I asked.

"No," she replied. "Far too expensive."

That night I passed the stone. I was by this time quite certain that what had been causing me so much pain and grief in its passage down the tube from kidney to bladder must possess the dimensions and contours of a jagged half brick. In the event the object which, in the middle of a stream of urine, came pinging out into our leaking loo, was roughly the size of a grain of caster sugar.

I was so ashamed that I flushed it down the Majorcan sewers.

Scrap

The family was nothing if not consistent when it came to choosing names. "The Old Man" who started the business, and whom I knew for a short time before he died, was called Harry. When he had a son, who eventually took over the business, they called him Harry. So what could be more natural than, when Harry Junior came to have a son, that they should call him Harry. One might have thought that such uniformity would have led to some confusion, but everyone knew that if you asked for Harry you meant the current boss.

They owned a scrap yard. Harry's son drove the lorry, and his daughter kept house, as their mother had died some years ago. Harry sat in his caravan in the middle of the yard surrounded by heaps and piles and loads and mountains of scrap: old baths, cars, pipes, bedsteads, batteries, stoves and cranes lay in chaotic abandon.

"How do you know where anything is when you want it?" I asked him one day.

"I knows," he replied cryptically.

"Is all that mess worth anything, Harry?"

"There's a bloody fortune out there," he said, and I believed him.

"Bloody," was the only epithet he knew. He used it as adjective or adverb, and scattered it indiscriminately throughout his conversation. It was sometimes a word of approbation, sometimes of stricture, and sometimes it was used purely for its euphonic effect. Only the context and the emphasis applied allowed one to identify in what sense it was being used on any particular occasion.

His yard lay next to the main road and bore no sign or board to identify it. None was needed. Everyone knew where Harry's yard was. But one day as I was driving past, I noticed that the word "Scrap" in huge white letters had been painted on the side of a rusty crane overlooking the road. I knew Harry could not have been responsible for the sign himself as, although it was not widely known, the truth was that Harry could neither read nor write. Anyway, there it was making its announcement to the world, until, inevitably, the temptation to the local youth proved too much. I noticed that a large splodge of white paint had been applied to the initial letter, obliterating it, and leaving the other four conspicuously shouting their scatalogical message to the passing motorists. Harry, of course, in his illiterate innocence, remained unaware of this salacious publicity, and I was not going to be the one to tell him. It was the local council I suspect, feeling that it detracted from the good repute of the district, who eventually had the offensive letters rendered illegible with a further application of white paint.

Harry insisted on being a private patient. In his book this gave him the right to circumvent the secretarial barrier, and ring me at home at any time of day or night to demand my services. He never came to see me at the surgery. After a consultation he would ask: "What's the damage, doc?" Taking a thick roll of filthy bank notes, secured with a rubber band, out of his hip pocket. I would suggest a modest sum by way of a fee. "That's not e-bloody-nough," he would complain, peeling another couple of notes off the roll. (This trick of interpolating "bloody" between syllables of one word was one of his favourite idioms.) "'Ere, buy the Duchess a new 'at," he would add, carelessly elevating my wife to the peerage as he pressed the notes into my hand.

On one of my last visits to him I noticed – and it was hard not to notice it – a spanking new Rolls Royce parked by a mound of scrap.

"What's that doing here, Harry?" I asked.

"Always promised myself one of them bloody Rollers when I'd earned myself a bob or two," he replied.

I saw it several times after that, always parked in the same place and no sign of it ever having been moved.

It was there when he died. I don't think he ever drove it.

Shep

Today "Double Barn" is a smart residence – a wealthy couple, with a B.M.W. and a Land Rover parked in the driveway. Forty years ago it was no more than it said it was: a double barn. One half of it gave shelter to hay or silage, and in the other lived "Shep" Phillips, one of the last of the Downland shepherds, with his two dogs.

The accommodation was sparse. Shep occupied two rooms in one of which he slept on a ramshackle bed, with his dogs on their straw bedding beside him. The other was furnished with a sturdy rough wooden table, two or three chairs and a large old-fashioned black kitchen range. The floor was of bare brick, and the door, operated by a simple thumb latch, was ill-fitting and quite incapable of excluding draughts in summer, let alone the bitter winds of winter. When it rained water seeped under the threshold.

Whatever the shortcomings of his dwelling, Shep's garden was immune from criticism. Devoted entirely to the cultivation of vegetables, it could have fed half the city with beans, marrows, onions, carrots, parsnips and potatoes, all of imperial size and sovereign quality.

My wife and I had just started to grow a few vegetables in a small patch outside our back door and I mentioned to Shep that I had planted some potatoes and the carrots were just appearing above the soil.

"Don't touch them 'taters till the 'aulms be dyin'," he said, "and them carrots will get the fly' less you treads 'em," he added. "Like this 'ere," and he walked slowly along the brick floor of his kitchen putting the heel of one of his thick-soled boots in front of the toe of the other, in a straight line.

I went home and conscientiously walked heel to toe along the thin green line just as he had shown me.

It was our first attempt at growing vegetables, and it soon became obvious that the seedlings that I had so carefully protected from the ravages of carrot fly, were in fact beans.

Next time I went to see Shep I made a full confession of my stupidity. I thought it might amuse him, but nothing had prepared me for the hurricane of hilarity that my tale provoked: the rib-splitting guffaws and the rolling of his eyes in stupefied amusement that this supposedly clever, educated young doctor did not know the difference between a line of carrots and a row of broad beans. When his laughter eventually subsided sufficiently to allow him to wipe the tears from his eyes, I said "Well Shep, at least they didn't get the carrot fly!" That started him off again: gales of merriment almost throwing him out of his chair with the violence of the convulsions.

I have often wondered since whether the experience contributed to the severe stroke he had a couple of weeks later.

Sir John

There have never been many members of the medical hierarchy who have commanded my unreserved respect. A medical knighthood makes the cynical rank and file wonder how many committees the recipient must have chaired to have earned the distinction. A peerage, the ultimate accolade of the establishment, arouses deeper suspicions. There are however some colleagues who have been honoured for excellence in their own field of medical practice. They are few, but they are readily identified by the profession, who rejoice that their work has been publicly recognised.

One such was Sir John. I had heard him spoken of with universal respect throughout my student days and my early years in practice by all sections of the profession. Abreast of every advance in his speciality, initiating many himself, he nevertheless managed to retain the wisdom and balanced outlook essential in anyone who truly deserves the title of consultant. He enhanced the practice of medicine, which Sir William Osler once described as: "An art, not a trade; a calling, not a business; a calling in which your heart will be exercised equally with your head. Courage and cheerfulness will not only carry you through the rough places of life, but will enable you to bring comfort and help to the weak-hearted, and will console you in the sad hours, when, like Uncle Toby, you have to 'whistle that you may not weep'."

I never thought to meet him, but long after he had retired, a widower, old and frail, nearly blind and tired of life, he came to live with, and be cherished by his daughter, who was a patient of mine. I used to visit him occasionally. He liked to talk of old days, of the practice of medicine as he saw it, and always of how tired he was. He was waiting placidly for death.

One day he developed pneumonia and I was called to see him. He knew he was seriously ill. I asked him what he would like me to do for him.

"I'm so tired," he said. "Would you give me a quarter of morphia?"

I swallowed hard. A quarter of a grain of morphia (he had used the old standard of dose measurement) would indeed give him the rest he craved, but might very well kill him. I suppose I should have ridiculed his request and given him an injection of an antibiotic instead. Yet I could not help feeling that had our roles been reversed he would not have hesitated.

"Of course, Sir John," I said, "I'll give you some morphia."

I took his daughter aside, told her what he had asked, and what I had decided to do, having explained the danger involved. She listened carefully and agreed.

I left the house with a strange mixture of guilt, and elation that I had been able to be a friend to a senior colleague for whom I had always had the deepest respect.

Next morning, with some apprehension, I returned to the house. I found him sitting up in bed enjoying a good breakfast.

"The best night's sleep I've had for a long time," he said.

Some weeks later he died peacefully in his sleep.

The Brethren

"Do you mind if I have a cigarette?"

My question was greeted by one of those silences which leaves one in no doubt that it would have been better left unasked. I had the impression that I had asked the Chief Rabbi for a ham sandwich.

"There'll be no smoking in this house. We are of the Brethren," came the eventual reply.

They were a farming family I had previously had very little to do with, but I had been called in the middle of the night to attend one of their daughters who had developed acute appendicitis. I was hanging on the telephone trying to speak to the appropriate doctor at the hospital, and had felt the need of a cigarette. This was before the days when smoking became medically and socially unacceptable, but the family were, I quickly discovered, Members of the Plymouth Brethren: no music, no television, reading of the Bible and improving literature only, and certainly no smoking. I made my apologies, and a mental note of their principles to avoid making future remarks which might offend, and we parted on friendly terms.

Months, possibly a year or two, later, the daughter who had had appendicitis, came to the surgery.

"Would you give me a certificate to show my father to say that I am a virgin?" she asked, This was an unusual request, even thirty years ago, and I had to ask her why he was in need of such assurance.

"I have been out with a boy. We have done no more than kiss each other, but my father is unwilling to believe me; he insists that we marry, and I'm not sure I want to marry him."

Having carried out the necessary examination I was able to supply her with the certificate she required.

A few days later I was called to the farmhouse as her mother was in acute distress. It was apparent that an unholy (if that word is appropriate in such a household) row was in progress. Father was confronting the young couple insisting that they got married. "They may not have lain together, but their flesh has been joined," he said.

A few weeks later I heard that they had got married. The parents had sold the farm and moved with the other daughter to be "nearer to a suitable place of worship."

Years passed and then I was stopped in one of the city streets by a young couple with a baby in a push-chair.

"Do you remember us?" the mother asked. The last time I had seen her was in tears confronting her inflexible father.

"We've been married four years now, and we are very happy," she said.

The Buck Stops Where?

Prior to David's Steel's Bill of 1967, abortions were undoubtedly carried out not only in back streets, but by reputable surgeons in respectable N.H.S. hospitals. It was Alec Bourne, a consultant gynaecologist, who in 1938, performed a termination of pregnancy on a fourteen year old girl, who had been raped by guardsmen. He announced to the press that he was going to perform this operation, as he regarded it as a matter of principle and wished it to be treated as a test case. He was duly arrested and brought to trial, where he pleaded that the continuation of pregnancy in such circumstances was a threat to the patient's health, that life depends on health and, if health is sufficiently impaired, death results; that as it was legal to terminate a pregnancy to save life, he had therefore acted within the law. This argument was accepted.

The 1967 Act was intended to remove doubts about the legality of abortion under certain circumstances. Those who drafted the bill performed semantic gymnastics to prevent it being interpreted as abortion on demand. Subsequent events have proved their efforts to have been unsuccessful.

Shortly after the passage of the 1967 Act, when its clauses were interpreted rather more strictly than they are now, I was consulted by a young mother who had a child aged three. A year ago her husband had left her and a boyfriend had moved in. She had recently become pregnant by him and immediately after he discovered this he had left her. Her husband heard that she was alone again and had sought a rapprochement.

The mother told me that she had never ceased loving her husband, and that she longed for them to be together again, but she was positive that he would never be able to accept that she was carrying another man's child. If he found out he would refuse to come back to live with her. Would I please arrange for her pregnancy to be terminated?

The only clause of the Act which I could invoke was that the continuation of the pregnancy would "afford a substantial risk of injury to her mental health." This would have to be supported by a second opinion. The act says nothing about the continuation of the pregnancy affording "a substantial risk of ruining a potentially happy reconciliation of a married couple with a young child."

I wonder what the lawyers would have done if they had been in my position?

The Carmelite

It was the usual story. She had been digging in the garden, gone to bed with a bit of a back-ache, and now, next morning, she could hardly stand upright.

I examined her, told her that she had strained her back, and if she were to stay in bed for two or three days all would be well. But, I explained, she must have a board under the mattress to keep her back straight and prevent it "sagging." I went through my usual routine of describing the required size, thickness and shape of the board, and where it must be positioned in the bed, and ended my piece by apologising.

"It may sound a bit monastic," I said, "But, in fact you should find it quite comfortable."

At this point I saw her smiling and winking at her husband who was grinning from ear to ear, "The doctor doesn't know the joke does he?" she said.

"Indeed I don't. What's so funny?"

She replied: "For fifteen years before I was married I was a Carmelite nun living in a convent. For those fifteen years I slept on a straw palliasse on bare boards. I don't think I shall find your board too much of a hardship, doctor."

The Gladstone Bag

My arithmetic tells me that it was over eighty years ago that my mother and I went shopping in the luggage department of Harrods, but I can still recall every detail of the expedition.

I was about to start my first term at prep school, and it was mandatory that I should be equipped with a trunk, a tuck box and an overnight, or "last minute," bag. Suitable specimens were selected, and orders given for my name to be inscribed on the first two in black paint, in order to identify them from the almost identical items of those who were shortly to be my schoolmates. The overnight bag, being smaller, merely had to have my initials impressed on one side. All were delivered within a day or two, accurately inscribed, to our flat by one of those green electric Harrods delivery vans, alas no longer seen.

I imagine that the reason for my remembering this occasion in such detail was in part that I was experiencing the natural apprehension of going to boarding school for the first time, but also because, for the second time in my life, I was shortly to be faced with the prospect of not seeing my mother again for two years. She was off to rejoin my father supporting the British Raj in India.

In these days of child protection, social workers and counselling, it is hard to understand how before the war my brother and I, along with thousands of other "Orphans of the Empire," were regularly handed over to the care of others, while our parents went to all corners of the globe to ensure that the British Empire was efficiently administered. There were no "lollipop specials" conveying children out by jet aeroplane to rejoin parents for school holidays. I saw my mother for six months in every two years, and my father for six months in every four. In the interim, when not at school, we were cared for by grandparents, by aunts and in foster homes. Not everyone was as lucky as we were, as Rudyard Kipling so eloquently testifies about his own experiences.

It was sad enough for us, the children, but what must it have been like for the parents to suffer the agony of these severances of family ties repeated throughout their working lives? I think they must have been comforted by a feeling of a duty being fulfilled. They were under an obligation to carry "The White Man's Burden," and were called upon, as members of what many of them undoubtedly thought of as the greatest nation in the world to carry the message to others, and so keep Britain great. Family life took second place to this duty.

The overnight bag was essential because, while the trunk and tuck-box were sent "P.L.A.," (Passenger's Luggage in Advance. 2/- per item collected or delivered, 2/6d per item collected and delivered), the bag was for "last minute" indispensables, e.g. tooth paste, pyjamas, slippers and hair brush, which could not be sent in advance.

My bag was of the orthodox "Gladstone" shape: a flat firm base, each end triangular, and the sides meeting in a clasp at the top, all in genuine leather. It was of modest dimensions, about 15 inches long, and 6 inches high and wide. It served me faithfully throughout my schooldays, and was then pensioned off, a bit battered, to lie gathering dust in the attic for many years.

It was not resurrected until I started in general practice and had need of a doctor's bag in which to keep stethoscope, torch, prescription pad, blood pressure machine etc., and for this it proved ideal. For thirty years it accompanied me on my rounds, becoming a little more patched and stained as time progressed; it even suffered the indignity of a replacement handle made of plastic. However, of all the scars it bore none was more honourable than the two vicious puncture wounds penetrating one end.

Miss Sharp lived in part of an old Victorian house approached by a drive. When walking up the drive one could spot, in a small shrubbery to one side, three small headstones. These bore the inscriptions "Jock," "Bob" and "Ben," and, after each name, the letters "O.E S." and a date. On arriving at the house any question there may have been in one's mind as to the meaning of the inscriptions was answered by the fierce barking and baring of the teeth of what could only be an Old English Sheepdog. "Don't worry, doctor. He's only noise," Miss Sharp would say by way of reassurance, as I thankfully watched her lead him off into the next room.

One day Miss Sharp was taken seriously ill and, instead of receiving me in her sitting room, was confined to bed. As I approached the house the unrestrained O.E.S. came bounding out, hackles raised, eyes blazing, snarling through his bared teeth. I wasted no time and turned to run for the sanctuary of my car. A moment before I reached my goal he leapt at me. I was just able to interpose my bag between his jowl and the seat of my trousers before he struck, sinking his incisor teeth into the ancient leather. Panting with exhaustion and relief in the car I heard Miss Sharp's mellow tones floating down the driveway from her bedroom window: "Don't worry, doctor. He's only noise."

The Pill

It was shortly after the previous Pope had issued his uncompromising encyclical: "Humanae Vitae," in 1968, forbidding all forms of contraception other than the rhythm method, (dubbed by the less devout: "Roman Roulette") that Jeanette came to my surgery. She must have been about eighteen and unmarried. She had the hesitant approach, characteristic of one who is having to cope with a problem causing personal embarrassment.

"I think I may be pregnant, doctor."

I knew her family to be practising Roman Catholics, and I also knew that her church dealt particularly sympathetically with the predicament that Jeanette found herself in. Nevertheless, when examination confirmed her fears she was understandably greatly distressed.

"Have you been taking any precautions?" I asked her.

"Yes, doctor," she replied, as if in the confessional, "I have been taking the pill."

"That is usually very effective. Are you sure you have been taking it every day?" I asked.

"Religiously, doctor," she replied.

Undertakers

Undertakers are always good for a laugh. In plying their trade they show enormous respect and consideration for their clients (or, more accurately. to their clients' next of kin), in an effort to, in some way, mitigate the sadness of the events which have made their services necessary. Yet the border line between the respectful and the macabre is very finely drawn. On one occasion when visiting one of their establishments to identify 'the deceased', I noticed that it seemed to be unusually full of clients awaiting attention.

"Have you been busy lately, Mr. Wood?" I asked innocently.

"It's been murder," he replied. Not a shadow of a smile crossed his features.

The same gentleman had the misfortune to fall into one of his own graves in the course of satisfying himself that it had been dug to the required depth. I met him a few days later and he obviously thought it the funniest thing that had ever happened.

"Nearly did it that time, doctor. Broke three ribs, I did."

Roars of laughter followed this announcement, cut short by a painful grimace and clutching of the broken bones.

"My men wanted to make a job of it and cover me up there and then." More guffaws and painful contortions.

It used to be the custom, and I dare say still is in some parishes, that while the parishioners were buried in the churchyard with their feet facing to the east, a priest was laid to rest facing the opposite way, so that on the Day of Judgement, when they rose from their graves, the parishioners found themselves confronted by their priest. Thus, facing his flock, he was better able to remind them of the admonitions he had given them while they were still on earth.

The increasing popularity of cremation must have made this custom largely irrelevant, except, that is, to one undertaker about whom our vicar told me. He was a very modern man, who, I am sure, would have preferred to be known as a mortician rather than an undertaker, and was fully versed in the niceties of the disposal of the dead.

"Tomorrow, sir," he said to the vicar, "we have the sad duty of arranging for the cremation of the late Rev. Jack Robinson. As he was a Clerk in Holy Orders, sir, is it your wish that his body enters the furnace feet first, instead of head first, as is the custom with the laity?"

The vicar's reply was suitably deflating.

Our most dramatic incident concerning undertakers might well have turned out to be a cause célèbre. The inside of the church was being redecorated by some workmen, and the vicar had warned them that a funeral would be held that afternoon, and had asked them to cease work during the service as a measure of respect. When the cortège entered the church they dutifully laid aside their brushes and paint, and remained silent until the service had finished.

It was a burial, and those pieces of wood upon which the coffin rests before being lowered into the grave, (known by the euphonious name of 'putlocks'), had just been withdrawn. The coffin was slowly disappearing below ground and the relatives were standing by the graveside. Suddenly a voice said, "That's not Aunt Nellie."

As the coffin was being lowered the plaque bearing the name of the occupant had become visible, and indeed it was not that of Aunt Nellie.

Naturally enough, confusion and embarrassment ensued. Eventually the coffin was replaced in the hearse and conveyed back to the funeral parlour with unseemly haste, there to be exchanged for the one containing the elusive Aunt Nellie. She, of course, had not only been usurped in her grave, but had so far been denied a church service. So, with due solemnity her coffin was carried to the church and the cortège reformed.

The painters, who sometime previously had reapplied themselves to their task, were a little surprised to find their work again interrupted. The vicar had said nothing about there being two funerals that afternoon. Their immediate surprise was as nothing compared with their astonishment when they recognised the mourners were exactly the same as those in the first funeral. What sort of game was the vicar playing at?

Some weeks later I mentioned this drama to the manager of the undertakers concerned.

"It was a nightmare, sir. Brings me out in a sweat to think of it. You see sir, the other body was for cremation that afternoon, and if we hadn't caught it in time they could have taken us to the cleaners."

Ways and Means

Years before holistic medicine was fashionable, general practitioners and the clergy used to co-operate as each recognised that many problems were composed of both physical and spiritual elements. There was therefore an important, but limited two-way traffic between the surgery and the vicarage. On occasions help was sought from the wrong shop.

The vicar stopped me in the street one morning:

"A patient of yours came to see me the other day, but I'm afraid I couldn't be of much help to him."

"I'm sure you did what you could. What was his problem?"

"He was very worried that he was impotent."

"How did he think that you could help?"

"I don't know, but I lent him a book on theology. I thought it might stiffen his resolve, if nothing else."

Wrong Orifice

There are few complaints more annoying to patients or to doctors than nosebleeds. What should be a trivial incident easily corrected, can very easily develop into a messy, demoralising catastrophe for the patient, and a frustrating problem for the doctor.

The very great majority of nosebleeds originate from a small area at the front of the nose below the boney bridge. There is only one effective first-aid measure to stop the bleeding. Forget about cold keys down your back, or lying down with a flannel held over the bridge of your nose. Blow your nose over a basin to expel the blood and clots, then sit in an upright chair and immediately pinch the soft part of the nose firmly between fore-finger and thumb, and keep it pinched for a good five minutes. This should be timed by the clock, as five minutes is a long time to hold your nose. Meanwhile keep your mouth open or you will suffocate.

Like many other events in life patients with nosebleeds seem to occur in clusters: none for months and then three in a week. One of my colleagues had been plagued with a veritable epidemic of requests to visit bleeding noses. The latest in the series occurred in the small hours.

"Sit your wife up, pinch her nose and keep pinching it until I arrive," he instructed the distraught husband on the other end of the telephone.

When he pulled up at the house he was annoyed to find the husband standing outside waiting for him.

"I thought I told you to keep pinching your wife's nose until I arrived," he said.

"I tried that doctor, but it didn't seem to work. I think my wife's having a miscarriage."